WITHDRAWN

Ground Fog and Night

Poetry by Eugene J. McCarthy

Other Things and the Aardvark

Ground Fog and Night

Ground Fog and Night

POEMS BY EUGENE J. McCARTHY

 Harcourt Brace Jovanovich, New York and London

To the memory of Robert Lowell

Some of these poems appeared originally in
Harper's Magazine and *Ladies' Home Journal*.

Library of Congress Cataloging in Publication Data

McCarthy, Eugene J   1916—
Ground fog and night.

I. Title.
PS3563.A259G76   811'.5'4   78-11437
ISBN 0-15-137261-6

First edition

B C D E

Contents

Ground Fog and Night

The Book of Yeats

A Book of Yeats, she gave to me.
"Read this," she said, and think no more of you and me.

I sat and read, and read,
with bowed head,
while the waiting years
rustled at my ears,
shoving and pushing for a place
upon my narrow shoulder blades,
like vultures on too small a branch.

And then I said,
"We who together the great gazebo built
and struck the match and blew the flame
to burn time down
will live on now in curtained rooms
and let time grow as rank
as tamarack in a swamp,
all green below while dying at the top.

"And we who watched the moon stagger
across the sky
and drank its mad light and danced
to all its phases
will come on dark nights, alone,
when only owls can see and blind moles
mate and move.

"And we who together laughed at Anne Gregory's hair
and changed its color to our own desire
will think no more of chestnut or of yellow,
or laugh together, or new texts contrive.

3

"And we who played—
you the trout turned
glimmering girl,
and I the Aengus
following, desperate,
through hollow and through hilly lands,
the chase ending at last
in long dappled grass—
will walk only in flat places,
separate, yet within each other's sight,
like fixed stars, in a parking lot,
our light slowly dying.

"And we who heard the curlew . . ."

"Put down the book," she cried.
"Give me your hand and rest
your head upon my breast."

Then all the bare-necked birds
flew off my back.

The Needed Word

Always it is there
And then lost.
Between the night and the veil
Of whitening morning light
And then again
In the shadows of dusk.

We pursue it,
Riding pale horses
Among the aspen trees.
Or as rider and ridden,
Last centaurs among
Elm and oak.

We seek it as diggers
In one more cave,
Where bats flutter
And hang upside down.
Seeking the one last gospel,
Not found
Seeking the needed word,
Needed.

Three Poems about Cows

MARC CHAGALL

When I met Marc Chagall
I asked him first of all
whether he had ever seen
in life or in a dream
a cow just sitting down.
He said that he had seen
cows both blue and green
and also that he knew
cows that danced and cows that flew
but that he had never seen
in life or in a dream
a cow just sitting down.

THE COW

The cow is a very strange beast.
Because of missing upper teeth
it cannot bite or eat directly,
therefore it ruminates.
It has several stomachs.
When it lies down
it does one half at a time,
first the front, then the rear.
When it gets up
it does the reverse,
first the rear, then the front.
Since this is its way
a cow never voluntarily sits down.

MOON SHOT

Dedicated to the Manned Spacecraft Center

There once was a cow.
Do not ask how
but when bit by a fly
she jumped so high
she hurdled the moon.
As she went over
she searched for clover
and when she found none
she said, "I'd as soon
Be in Houston."

The Camera

I prove life
I prove death

I condemn
I pardon

I animate
I paralyze

I bind
I loosen

I reduce
I enlarge

I fix beauty
I hold ugliness

My eye is everywhere.
I am Tom, peeping

Through the crack in the door,
Under the drawn curtain.

I am the great eye
Looking around the curve of the earth.

I have seen both sides of the moon.
I have seen the depths of the sea.

Cowards turn brave in my beam.
Heroes in action cease fire.

Savage and sage fear me.
"No pictures, please."

Popes and potentates stand
At my call "Hold it" and "Smile."

My power is in deep darkness
In a womb of emulsion

Where eggs of silver
Wait for sudden light.

No seven days of creation,
No nine months' gestation.

But now and forever. Amen.

Handwriting

The wind blows through your letters.
It draws the dots on i's like smoke
    from east to west.
It tilts the t's but does not bend the b's.
It whispers through the double s's.
It flattens a's and r's.
It puffs up q's and u's.
It sounds most roundly in the o's
and is most gentle with the m's,
especially in your name.
Only the y's, like weathervanes,
point against the wind
to show where it came from.

Tuesday

I am afraid on Tuesday.
Tuesday can be lost
Between Monday and Wednesday,
Chewing each other
Like the blue lips
of the toothless hound.

Wednesday

Today, I will walk all the roads,
All the paths of the world.
I will work at plowing and planting,
Help with harvests.
I will build houses and barns,
Make hinges and handles,
Tables and chairs.
I will untangle yarn,
And watch weavers at work,
Pick apples in old orchards,
Bless abandoned farms,
And all places where hollyhocks
Show that gardens once grew.
I will write a poem,
Before it is Thursday.

No Country for the Young

This is no country for the young.
Vultures prey on living flesh
and eat the skins off kettledrums.
The old refuse to die.

Eyes turn inward, chicken-like,
or stare, unlidded, vague as fish
within a deep and pressuring sea.

At the St. Regis
ice cubes smell of mammoth flesh,
and all the clocks have stopped.
A three-fingered pianist
plays only the black keys
until the dancers fall.
Shadows dare to stand against a sun
veiled by the ash of Hiroshima.

Time is tired of you and me.
It now runs out
like dust
from the broken hourglass.

The young begin too soon
to wait to be the last.
They cover stains of salt and blood
with antimacassars
and watch old curtains disintegrating
from the bottom up.

My Lai Conversation

How old are you, small Vietnamese boy?
Six fingers. Six years.
Why did you carry water to the wounded soldier, now dead?
Your father.
Your father was enemy of free world.
You also now are enemy of free world.
Who told you to carry water to your father?
Your mother!
Your mother is also enemy of free world.
You go into ditch with your mother.
American politician has said,
"It is better to kill you as a boy in the elephant grass
      of Vietnam
Than to have to kill you as a man in the rye grass
      in the USA."
You understand,
It is easier to die
Where you know the names of the birds, the trees,
      and the grass
Than in a strange country.
You will be number 128 in the body count for today.
High body count will make the Commander-in-Chief
      of free world much encouraged.
Good-bye, small six-year-old Vietnamese boy, enemy of
      free world.

A Short Book of Trees

Elm and oak keep decent distances.
Pine and hickory
Crowd and grow in thickets.
Willows are often found
Where they should not be.
They tell of water,
Of old wells and springs,
Both deep and shallow.
Lombardy poplars grow fast in suburbs.
They outlive the sudden people of their planting.
Basswood, like box elders, are found in groves.
They are not much for headlands
And should be kept near bees.
The cottonwood, revered by Indians,
Does not know enough to come in from the cold
Or stay away from river floodlands.
The maple is arrogant.
Now used for rake handles,
It remembers better days
As shaft of lance and spear.
Beech trees are ghostly but truthful.
Their bark will tell
Who loved whom for years.
Apple trees are good
For fruit and holding scythes.
Some trees will not leave home.
Lilacs and sumac stay behind
When houses leave
And lanes are overgrown.

The Fountain

Gently the love laughter
    of water is sounded.
Brightly on wet stones
    light is compounded.

Grace notes sprung
    free flung, faith hung.

Now falling
    down, down, down.

Fountains are futile.
    All fountains fail.

Robert Frost

I

You are an old cow
feeding on overgrazed pasture
of bluegrass and timothy.
You shuttle your head through barbed wire
reaching for sweeter fodder and forbidden weeds.
You drive off critical flies with a slash
of your tail
or more selectively with a forward kick.
Ruminant, you chew a cud of words,
nodding always at questions,
you who have asked yourself all
and answered.

II

You are an old tree,
black maple, on a north slope,
growing clear without shoots or suckers,
like basswood or box elders.
Your knuckled roots hold rocks
deep in the thin soil.
The word sap rises in you,
is drawn off and burned down.
You throw it hot onto the snow.
Pure words form in the cold.
"There you are," you say.
"Now let the green leaves come."

III

You are a Model T painted black.
The choke wire sticks out of the radiator.

16

The crank hangs in a sling.
Starting you is not easy.
The spark must be set right,
the magneto coils dry.
Your kick can break a man's arm.
On cold days one may have to jack up
one of your hind wheels
to get you started.

Once started you are dangerous.
You are always slightly in gear.
Your brakes are marginal.
There is risk in riding with you.
Your fuel tank is under the front seat.
You run on gasoline or on kerosene.
Either can explode.

You are not exactly comfortable.
You have leaf springs but no shock absorbers.
Your tires have inner tubes
and are not puncture proof.
You carry no spare tire,
only tire tools and patching.

Because your fuel system depends on gravity,
not on a vacuum,
you climb steep hills in reverse.
You provide sure passage in spring mud,
have clearance enough for pasture rocks
and for the center ridge of deep rutted roads.

Your fenders carry small boys.
Your running boards are lined with poets.
You get us there.

17

Nine Horses

Numbered in green paint,
Nine horses in a row.
Sore-footed, spavined,
Heads hung low,
They ignore, as they go,
Cars and lights,
And right of way.

Nobody knew their names.
When busy as the poor, they moved,
Under the hammer of the auctioneer,
Lifting their feet too high,
As the old, dancing in jumps,
Prove they are alive.

Do they remember high plateaus,
Stallions and wild mares with foal,
Percheron meadows, the weight
Of knights in armor, great battles,
And later hunts and races?

The fear in white-eyed blindness
As cataract darkness pours
From the sky ahead of storms,
While heel chains and harness
Irons ring faster than all bells?

Is that half-blind Bucephalus,
Who knew the gentle thighs of Alexander?
And that, Pegasus, with saddle sores
Where once wings sprouted?
And those, the broken-winded ones,
The horses of Antara?

And that one, among them,
With shorter ears, and deeper eyes,
Remembering drumming hooves,
A neck curled, vain with
The mane cresting in the wind,
The sweetness of grass,
The caress of green water
In sliding nostrils,
The fierce movement
Of the loins
And also the taste
Of bread and of wine,
The reaching touch of hands
On the body of a woman?

Does the chest strain to be again
The trunk of man?

Only a cry escapes
Through the fast-growing teeth.
Surprise, surprise,
The last desperate cry,
Of the last centaur.

A Quota on Honey

Now a quota on honey
May seem very funny
To people who talk on TV.
But consider the tree
In need of a bee
To insure it posterity.
The standard Manhattan without a cherry
And no lemon peel for the dry Martini.
The empty hive, the exiled queen,
The disconsolate drone,
The last clover sown,
And in search of one flower
Ladybird wandering
Through the dismal, gray, desolate
Terminal spring.

No Deposit—No Return

Better be wanted dead or alive
Than be a bottle of "no deposit—no return."

The livery horse required a pledge.
The rental car at least a name.
Return postage is guaranteed
On free seed and third-class mail.

Slave ships captained
By men of God left glass beads
On the golden sand.
Bourbon barrels are reused,
Tin cans and old cars
Crushed into cubes
Sent to Japan.

Now leave her here at the nursing home.
She will have company
And continuous care.
No deposit, no return
On the bottle that once knew wine,
The body that once knew love.

For Marcel Marceau

He appears as we look at the dark stage
in a moment of light, the brother of Athena
from the head of Zeus, but dumb.

He holds in his hands, at arm's length, a box.
It is heavy.
The tendons of his elbows stand out.
His biceps knot under his skin.

He is afraid of the box—of what is in it.
He lowers it to the floor.
His back bends
like a pine tree being bowed by weight of vines.

Then he straightens slowly, his muscles easing.
He steps back one step,
looks over his shoulder as if to flee,
or to see if anyone is watching.

Then he kneels,
each joint surrendering in genuflection.
He reaches for the clasp on the box.
He touches it.

He draws his hand back as though it were burned.
He rubs the hand, and slowly reaches again,
takes hold of the clasp. His arm trembles
as though an electric current were passing through it.

He opens the box. Now, an ecstasy of surprise.
Birds fly out.
Others he lifts out in his hands.
He fondles them and tosses them into the air.

He leaps with joy
And then he too flies.
His arms have become wings.
They, he, and the birds turn and soar and dive.

He flies higher than the birds.
He dives more dangerously.
He turns more smoothly.
The birds attack him.

He runs to the box, kneeling again.
He reaches for the birds.
He catches one and puts it in the box.
And another. But now the first one escapes.

He reaches and flails at the birds, more and more slowly.
The mask that is his face changes.
It sags, hanging from the black outline of his eyes
and from the thin curls at his ears.

Now the birds leave.
There is a smell of hunting,
of opened gizzards, of grayness.
He fights at nothing, as in a nightmare.
Now he gets into the box.
Only his hands show, at the last.
They pull down the top, the lock clicks.
The light goes, the dark returns.

My Companion Orders Dinner

On reading a restaurant review

"To begin," she said, "I will have
trivial tripe with alabaster endive,
and three stalks of taut asparagus.
Then the flexible flounder
and two Côte d'Azurs, medium,
with lucid leek and petulant parsnip,
a tensile turnip, a complacent tomato
and a baked preternatural potato.

"I will have the 'plat' plain
and two 'jours,' preferably
Tuesday and Wednesday."
Then, with her head a-tilt
a little like a daffodil,
she said, "To drink
I will have the ambience cold,
and for dessert, a half decor."

Lionesses

I have thought today
Of Edith Sitwell's lioness,
Remembering it is a raging fire
Like the heat of the sun,
The flowering of amber blood and bone,
Rippling of bright muscles like a sea,
The rose prickles of bright claws.

　　But more.

Much more: of gold and of saffron,
Of a tawny stretching,
A turning of ropes,
The movement of sand
Toward the sea, slower than wind.
And among all of this
Amber, gold, yellow,
Lion-brown eyes, openness.

Lionesses let on a lot.

The Diagonal Dark Path

The diagonal dark path
ran across the park.
False grass beside it grew
and told all that it knew
of everyone who passed,
of every lad and lass
who lay upon it
in the night.

It ran beneath black walnut trees
that each June deceived
with promises of meat
but in the autumn held but dust
in worm-drilled hulls.

Beyond it stood the public school,
sealed summer sepulcher of heresy.
The coal shute beckoned those
who craved to know
how learning lived
behind locked doors
and dared the cellar dark
and creaking stairs to see
pale blackboards, books
lying like poisoned pigeons
on the floor, husks of flies
sucked dry by spiders
and bees with pollen-laden thighs,
their myriad eyes deceived by glass,
dead or dying on the window sills.

Temptation lurked
in outdoor toilets
padlocked to preserve until September
the janitorial purgation,
sandpapered and planed,
pale spots where once
the facts of life
and who loved whom were told.

On still nights, iron swings
clanged in the calm.
Dead children had come back to play,
old women said.

Each boy at twelve was dared
to walk at night the diagonal path,
not break and run.
Each step no faster than the first
to prove, to prove, he could.

A Fungus among the Pharaohs

End of the Curse

Dr. Dean of Dublin has determined:
Lord Carnarvon did not die,
As newspapers reported in 1923,
Of a mosquito bite that led to blood poisoning
Which in turn led to pneumonia.

Dr. Dean of Dublin has determined:
It was not the curse of Tutankhamen
That laid his lordship low,
Even though lights in Cairo's Continental Hotel
Did dim, go out at the moment of his death.

Dr. Dean of Dublin has determined:
That stirred from the dry droppings of bats
There was a fungus among the Pharaohs
That did in Lord Carnarvon;
Arthur Mace and George Benedite, as well.

Summer Rental

This is my abode until October.
This is a habitable house.
It is a ready house.
Whoever lived here
Left just ahead of me.
They left rubber bands and paper clips,
Stamp holders, letter openers,
And a scale for weighing the mail.

This house has been kept.
There are sachet bags and orange balls
With nutmeg in the drawers.
Summer slipcovers are on the chairs
And summer rugs upon the floors.

The people who lived here
Read Trollope and Defoe.
They left quietly and decently.
Death did not interrupt.
They left generations in cupboards
And in corner closets,
Family silhouettes on the walls
And great-grandfather's sword and cup.

There was no quick sale
Or sudden moving out.
They left only under
The duress of summer.

Margaret

She is very hard to find.
Her eyes are speckled,
Her nose is freckled,
Her hair between chestnut and brown.
Her smile is almost a frown.
She lives in a room full of posters and pictures
With a brindle dog and a calico cat
And a sand-colored gerbil that is really a rat.
Were it not for the windows and door
You could not tell a wall from the ceiling or floor.

She's a trout in the sun,
A fawn in the shade,
A chameleon, ever changing her color.

When asked to use an umbrella, she maintains
"I have had very little trouble with rain."

A Page of Short Poems

The Lonely:
    Amputated hands
    Seeking each other in soft grass.

Ending:
    I am tired of the moon, she said,
    Let us go in and turn on the TV.

The Ark:
    All the animals came to the ark
    With their mates and their metaphors
    Save the unicorn, which had no mate,
    And the aardvarks, which had no metaphors.

Mary:
    You are gray smoke
    In a blue vase.

Night after a Dull Day:
    The waxen day has melted into the sea.
    The deaf sexton tolls the curfew bell.
    James Reston chews his cud.
    Jacob and the Angel
    Prepare to wrestle to a draw.

The Death of the Old Plymouth Rock Hen

It was tragic when her time came
After a lifetime of laying brown eggs
Among the white of leghorns.
Now, unattractive to the rooster,
Laying no more eggs,
Faking it on other hens' nests,
Caught in the act,
Taken to the woodpile
In the winter of execution.

A quick stroke of the axe,
One first and last upward cast
Of eyes that in life
Had looked only down,
Scanning the ground for seeds and worms
And for the shadow of the hawk.
Now those eyes are covered
By yellow lids,
Closing from the bottom up.

Decapitated, she did not act
Like a chicken with its head cut off.
No pirouettes, no somersaults,
No last indignity.
Like an English queen, she died.
On wings that had never known flight
She flew, straight into the woodpile,
And there beat out slow death
While her curdled voice ran out in blood.

A scalding and a plucking of no purpose.
No goose feathers for a comforter.
No duck's down for a pillow.
No quill for a pen.
In the opened body, no entrail message for the haruspex.
Not one egg of promise in the oviduct.
In the gray gizzard, no diamond or emerald,
But only half-ground corn,
Sure evidence of unprofitability.

The breast and legs,
The wings and things,
The strong heart,
The pope's nose,
Fit only for chicken soup and stew.
And then in March, near winter's end,
When blooded and feathered wood is used,
The odor of burnt offerings
Above the kitchen stove.

The Critic

In a room in an apartment
Where the light breaks back
From other windows
A woman is writing criticism.

Through the closed door
With the one-way spyglass
I hear the drum
Roll of her typewriter.

Now there is silence.
Her hands rise from the keys.
She bites her lip.
Her eyes narrow.

The whole apartment waits.
The city pauses.
The knife of the guillotine holds its notch.

And now words break
In a thunder of keys,
An avalanche of words, behind the door.
Again the woman is writing criticism.

Eaton's Corrasable

To Elizabeth Siebenthall

Who would have expected seventy-three poems in a carton
Of Eaton's corrasable
"With a rag content
Of twenty-five percent"
And assurances that "you can erase
Without a trace,"
That "errors disappear like magic,"
That "the secret is in the surface."
Seventy-three poems
Including
     The Rise and Fall of the Goat
     The Color of Purple
     Blue Lake

The secret is not in the surface
Or in the rag content
Of twenty-five percent
In the seventy-three poems
In the carton of Eaton's corrasable.

The secret is in the poet.

Your Garbage Man

I am your garbage man.
Near the furnace
In the apartment basement
I am sitting in your old Victorian chair.

I know more than you think.
People die slowly,
A little bit at a time.
In some cases dying takes a lifetime.

Not everything you throw away
Goes straight to the crusher or to the incinerator,
Or to the scow, headed for the Atlantic.
Some things I keep for myself.
Some I sell.
Some I give to relatives or friends
Or to the Goodwill Industries.

Your old brown pants are mine now.
I can tell them from how you walked.
I am waiting for the coat and vest.

Things are not going well for you.
Your shoes are resoled.
Your shirt collars are turned.
There are spots on your old neckties.
Your grade of whiskey has gone down.
You are drinking house brands.
I find empty Geritol and Grecian Formula
Bottles in your trash.

According to the Environmental Protection Agency
Each American uses twenty-eight tons
Of materials a year.

I carry you away many times
Before the mortician does his job.

When the body dies
There is loss of weight.
What is lost then is carried
By Charon, the boatman.

Park Lane Hotel, Toledo, Ohio

*Newspaper notice: "The Park Lane Hotel
closed today."*

The Park Lane Hotel, Toledo, Ohio.
Conrad Hilton never slept there
or left his bedside reader.
Not even the Gideons have left their book.

Room two hundred and four.
Like other rooms, a bed,
a chest of drawers, a chair,
and a desk, bookcase,
with three shelves of books,
unlike the books in any other room.

For fiction lovers:
Faithful Shirley (copyright 1892, 1893, and 1899).
Also, *Lost, a Pearle,* and *Virgie's Inheritance,*
all by Mrs. George Sheldon.

The Main Chance, 1903, by Merideth Nicholson,
dedicated to D.K.N., "who," we are assured in
the foreword, "will remember and understand."

Woman of Spain, by Scott O'Dell.
This book was formerly the property of
the Toledo Home for the Hard of Hearing.

Battling Love and Faith, 1902,
by Mary V. Allen.

The Daughters of Anderson Crow, 1907,
by George Barr McCutcheon.

And for lovers of nonfiction:
The Memoirs of Barras, Member of the Directorate,
18th Fructidor to 18th Brumaire,
Year V to Year VIII, published in 1896.

Modern Eloquence, in V Volumes, published in 1903.
The standard for selection was "style," which may
be defined as "proper words in proper place."

Volume I of the *Life of Charles Dickens,* 1905,
by John Forster (ex libris John O'Day, of Boston).

Volume IV of *Health and Strength,*
by John Nelson Goltra, M.D., 1917 to 1925.
"Written to teach by games and sports, the great
lessons of life."

Volume II of the *Works of Shakespeare,*
The Kenneth Roberts Reader of 1908,
and Volumes VII and VIII
of the new *International Encyclopedia,*
published in 1927, from Didymus to Foraker
(Joseph Benson Foraker), governor and senator
from Ohio, who, according to the last entry, in
May 1914 announced that he would run again
for the Senate in order to clear himself of charges.

There is no report in Volume VIII as to whether
Foraker won or lost or cleared his name. It may
be in Volume IX, in some other room.

There were four pictures in the room:
one of the three Graces,
one of a lady with two wolfhounds,
and two prints, of wild flowers
of September and of October, annotated.

There is a new Hilton in Toledo.

39

The Blue Guitarist

You do not play things as they are
When you play upon the blue guitar.
Now play the truth,
The Bishop cried. People said, Yea, Yea, Amen.
And the judge said, Play,
And the bailiff, too,
And they called in the sheriff
And the National Guard.

The fingerman sighed
And drew a deep, deep breath.
Now he laid the guitar across his knees.
He tuned each string to a perfect pitch.
Then he bowed his head to the work ahead.
He said, I will play things on the blue guitar
Exactly as they are.

He played it high and he played it low.
He played it fast and he played it slow.
He played it round and he played it square.
He played it well done and he played it rare.
He played it thin and he played it fat.
He played it sharp and he played it flat.
He played it loose and he played it tight.
He played it left and he played it right.
He played it new and he played it old.
He played it hot and he played it cold.
He played it crooked and he played it straight.
He played it early and he played it late.

Then the Bishop cried,
Oh, play no more on the blue guitar,
No one wants to hear things as they are.
And the people said, Yea, Yea, Amen,
And the judge, and the bailiff,
The sheriff, and the National Guard,

Then the fingerman raised
His hand from the strings
And the blood dripped down from his fingertips.
He eyed the crowd with a terrible look
And he struck a chord never heard before
As he broke the neck of the blue guitar.

Orthodox Convention

MORNING

The sons of Levi now decree
The interchangeability
Of plastic casings
And the guts of goats
For kosher sausage.

AFTERNOON

The sons of Levi on rented skates
Cut the ice in figure eights
While Sarahs and Jesabels and Ruths
Walk the lobby in new pants suits.

EVENING

Since crows cry havoc in all seasons,
Why didn't Noah know
Better than to send a crow
To see if spring had come.

"Roaches Take Over New York City Buses"

—*New York Times*

Roaches are not afraid of time—
They live in electric clocks.
Roaches are not afraid of space—
They live in cracks.
So why be surprised to find them on buses?
They are not afraid of motion.
Moreover, there is roaches' work to be done on buses.
Removing crumbs,
Keeping the engines clean of grease.
And survival fare in plastic seat covers.

Roaches go where they are needed.
And as a spokesman for the Transit Co. said,
"It's not a problem unique to buses.
Once a roach settles in, he's as much at home
On a city bus as in a Park Avenue apartment."

"We urge any passenger who sees a roach,"
He added, "to get the number of the bus
And call us."

Einstein had nothing to say to roaches.

House Movers

House movers, among men, are not to be blest.
The house that has been moved is never at rest,
Jacked up on girders and rollers,
Pulled down the street, against the wishes
Of trees and telephone wires.

Its new foundations are never right,
Too high or too low.
The trees are all strangers,
Distant and nervous.
They shade the wrong places.
Neighboring houses frown,
Their windows stare in the wrong places,
There are blank walls where
There should be windows and doors.

And at the old site—
Houses left behind worry.
Why did it leave without notice?
Did it have something to hide?
Which of us will be next?
Better to have torn it down
Or let it die.

Elm trees, in the yard, lean the wrong way.
The willows hang round the abandoned well.
The sumac decently cover
The wound of the open cellar,
Filled with old mattresses,
Tin cans, and barbed wire.
Lilacs slowly close the unused road.

House movers are not to be blest.

Admiral Radford Crosses the Continental Divide

Admiral Radford crosses the Continental Divide
asleep at thirty-two thousand feet.
He dreams of blue water, of his ships
moving above the mountains of the Pacific.
He thinks of co-ordinates,
of trajectories, of parabolas,
of the slant-eyed mariners
set against his straight and hooded look,
their ships built
with plans stolen from the Germans,
the steel of their hulls
from the planned waste of America.
He will strike at dawn,
guns at the ready.

The plane lands. His wife
stirs him awake.
No smart salutes, no piping through salt spray,
no descent of uncertain iron stairs.
The accordion tube of the airport
reaches for him.
He is helped into his wheel chair.
His wife pushes him out of his dreams.

Reflections on J. L.

She was different among the women
in the drawing rooms of London,
among titled widows, mistresses, and wives.
She was different among the men,
dandied dukes and earls and lords
who publicly proposed, and poets
who spoke at length of Guinness.

"She is Scotch," they said, "and haughty."

She walked among tables and chairs
thigh free as in heather,
leaning a little as into a wind,
clearer eyed, looking through
planes of air to farther hills.

Her hands were strong with the knowledge
of linen and wool, and the leap of the loom.
She wore the colors of moor and of heath
and her hair was true raven.

Much truth is in the roots
under light-footed walking
among scant flowers.

"She is Scotch," they said, "and haughty."

London

Steady flow of cabs and clerks.
Careful about small things,
Dates of births and deaths,
Of foundings and of failings.
Of titles, qualifications, and credentials.
Ltd.   Inc.   Esq.
Shirtmakers to dead kings,
Milliners to headless queens,
Vintners to alcoholic princes,
Tobacconists to prince consorts,
Money changers for Germans or French,
Lending it for War or Peace.
Modulated, impartial. A city of service,
Keeping time and standards.

Mouse

Ah, he was there. I heard
The burr of his scurrying between the studdings,
The high cries of his little lust,
The shrieks of his small fears.

Ah, he was there. I saw
His shadow among the shadows
Circling the reach of faint light.

Now, in the bottom drawer,
Following my nose, I find his remains—
Five whiskers, the claws, and the end of his tail.

He who of all the beasts,
Except the swallow, is most unbiddable,
According to Pliny.

His body, unfit for food,
And causing oblivion if eaten,
According to Porta.

A "verie ravenour or greedigut"
Considering his "bigness,"
According to John Maplet (1567).

He lived most intently
His twoscore months and ten,
His heart beating
Five hundred strokes to the minute,
Thirty thousand to the hour.

A fierce interior life.
His blood pressure beyond measure.
His liver waxing and waning
With the mood of the moon,
According to Aelian.

Listening, touching, squeaking,
Tasting, watching, but beyond
All of these, smelling.

Rampant, he was, among odors,
His nose twitching, his whiskers shaking,
His olfactory faculties at full speed.

Now he has left five whiskers,
The claws, and the end of his tail.
And ah, yes, a roomful of odors.

A room filled at his death with his life.
Drawn through small nostrils, extracted,
Compacted, in the silk sack of his body,
The essences of cheese, of mold, of dry bread
Now released.

If we had but let him smell better—
Rose leaves, tarragon, mint, and wild thyme—
How sweet and sublime
Would the death odors be
To go with the five whiskers,
The claws, and the end of his tail.

The Great Green Suit

There once was a patriot named Cuneen
Who had a suit of unusual sheen
Combining mold, and mist, and shamrock green.

It was, without doubt, the greatest of tweeds.
Its woof was wool, its warp of Irish reeds.

It stood alone, without hanger or board.
It had strength to withstand night stick and sword.

It was loose at the shoulder for fighting the British.
It was full in the trouser for running in ditches.

Its color was such that for hiding in heather
There was nothing better, and as for the weather,

It was fine in the sun but much better in rain,
For it repelled water, and scarce showed a stain.

It was so marvelous in its variety
It could serve, in a pinch, as a hair shirt for piety.

Then a woman's derision
Brought about a decision

To send the suit to the cleaner to have it made lighter
And then to the tailor to have it made tighter.

When the call came on the first moonlit night,
Kept from the fight and also from flight
Because the suit was too tight, Cuneen,

Concealed in a thicket so as not to be seen,
Was found by the smell of the kerosene.

On the very next day at the moment of dawn
They hanged him on the courthouse lawn.

But they honored at death his last request
And he wore the green suit to his final rest.

To Austin Clarke

William Butler Yeats is dead,
Patrick Kavanaugh gone to his reward.
Old poets, young poets, poets,
Honor Austin Clarke.

He walks alone in Ireland,
Black hat, muffler, greatcoat,
Threadbare buttonholes,
Pale eyes smiling, white hair
Drifting down like smoke in a heavy day.
It is left to him
To be the tongue of Ireland.
Listen to him at the last.

"I've no quarrel with the poets.
I've outlived nearly all my old friends.
Most of them died of drink.
I was saved by a weak stomach.
Many of the younger ones have gone to America
To teach, to live. I've stayed here.

"I've no quarrel with the Church.
The Archbishop is an able man.
There are many able men in the Church.
There must be for it to last.

"I've no quarrel with the government.
Poets are not censored in Ireland.
Playwrights, novelists, yes.
Not poets. Indifference, perhaps.
Irish Broadcasting treats me well.
They pay me even when I don't go on.

52

"Once as a boy
I climbed the wall at Coole Park.
Through the trees, I saw Yeats, walking.
It was wonderful.

"Poets don't know much, but they try.
They try every way; blind as bats
And deaf as well, they fly.
They carve stone with bone,
Form steel with sand.
They fight like small boys
With their eyes shut.
Crying before they are hurt, but brave."

Men in Vows

I sing today
In praise of oath-bound men,
Harnessed and held in vows
To patient or impatient wives,
To flags, to ships, perhaps to God.
No battering at the gates,
No fierce assault,
No beating of high air,
No condor eye cast only downward,
No hawks dive through bluing air,
No blood on beak or talon,
No red-tipped feather floats
Down from their air to write
Fear on the earth.
Well within the walls, the hulls,
The cells, they brace
Against the centrifuge,
Holding the center while others
Swing in wider gyres
And beat against the outer limitations
Of our powers.
On wax-held wings, wary of the sun,
They circle on updrafts from low hills
And from flat fields.
Slowly up near life
And gently down to death.

Courage at Sixty

Now it is certain.
There is no magic stone,
No secret to be found.
One must go
With the mind's winnowed learning.
No more than the child's handhold
On the willows bending over the lake,
On the sumac roots at the cliff edge.
Ignorance is checked,
Betrayals scratched.
The coat has been hung on the peg,
The cigar laid on the table edge,
The cue chosen and chalked,
The balls set for the final break.
All cards drawn,
All bets called.
The dice, warm as blood in the hand,
Shaken for the last cast.
The glove has been thrown to the ground,
The last choice of weapons made.

A book for one thought.
A poem for one line.
A line for one word.

"Broken things are powerful."
Things about to break are stronger still.
The last shot from the brittle bow is truest.

Tumbleweed

The tumbleweed never gets
a decent burial.
Not even in a common grave
with leaves and straw,
never matted down
and turned to mulch.

But driven by the wind
it moves in uneven starts and stops,
like Indians being driven to
less hospitable ground.
A dried and arid spirit, swirling
with Dante's rejected souls.

The small seeds lost in flight,
abandoned like children of the poor.
(No phoenix here, no new plant
out of the death of old.)
Spread-eagled, at last,
against wire fence,
it slowly turns to dust.

Ground Fog and Night

A cloud is subtly woven over the field.
Day and night together beget the cataract film.
It holds, while the earth, with its burden
Of brush and of trees,
Of houses and steeples, sinks slowly.

Day songs die and night birds' songs
Are dampened by the fog.
Crescendos of cicadas cross
The prairies of the night
And then are gone in silence like the bison.
Ruminant stomachs yield their cuds
And tree frogs
Fall into green sleep.
Spiders lying upside down
Like Michelangelo on his back
Make a ceiling between themselves and God
Plants rid themselves of death
Spawned in them by the sun.
Burrowing beasts live on as before.
Shrews and moles shelter
In their dark world the hoard
Stolen from the light.

Now owl and vermin do contest.
No winners from the day.
Men in air-conditioned rooms set clocks
Against the night and wait for dawn.
No sign of God is left above the fog.
Only the red-eyed tower stands
To tell of life
Below.